DEFENSE!

BY TIM POLZER

NFL

P9-DNL-946

SCHOLASTIC INC.

New York   Toronto   London   Auckland

Sydney   Mexico City   New Delhi   Hong Kong

Photo Credits:

Front cover: (top left): David Stluka/AP Images; (right): Paul Jasienski/AP Images; (bottom left): Greg Trott/AP Images

Back cover: (top): Jim Mone/AP Images; (center): Paul Jasienski/AP Images; (bottom): Kevin Terrell/AP Images

Title page: (top left): David Stluka/AP Images; (right): Paul Jasienski/AP Images; (bottom left): Greg Trott

(3): David Drapkin/AP Images; (5 top): Evan Pinkus/AP Images; (5 bottom): Bill Kostroun/AP Images; (7 top): Paul Abell/AP Images; (7 bottom): Morry Gash/AP Images; (8): Paul Spinelli/AP Images; (11 top left): Thomas E. Witte/AP Images; (11 top right): Paul Jasienski/AP Images; (11 bottom): Paul Spinelli/AP Images; (12): Paul Jasienski/AP Images; (13): Tom DiPace/AP Images; (14): Paul Jasienski/AP Images; (15): Kevin Terrell/AP Images; (17): Evan Pinkus/AP Images; (18): Carlos Osorio/AP Images; (21 top): Greg Trott/AP Images; (21 bottom): Carlos Osorio/AP Images; (22): Carlos Osorio/AP Images; (23): Paul Spinelli/AP Images; (25): Paul Spinelli/AP Images; (26): Ed Reinke/AP Images; (27): Paul Spinelli/AP Images; (28): Greg Trott/AP Images; (30): Kevin Terrell/AP Images; (31): Greg Trott/AP Images; (32): David Stluka/AP Images

ISBN 978-0-545-34639-9

12 11 10 9 8 7 6 5 4 3 2 1   11 12 13 14 15 16/0

Designed by Cheung Tai
Printed in the U.S.A.   40
First printing, September 2011

Clay Mathews

**G**reen Bay Packers linebacker Clay Matthews made the biggest play of his career in Super Bowl XLV. With the Packers holding a small lead in the fourth quarter, Matthews burst through the Pittsburgh Steelers offensive line and forced running back Rashard Mendenhall to fumble. The turnover prevented the Steelers from scoring and added to the Packers' lead. When the final seconds of the game counted down, Matthews and his teammates celebrated the Packers' first NFL championship in 14 years.

It's easy to see how playing professional football has always been a dream for Matthews. Football and the NFL have always been a big part of his family life. The Matthews family's professional football history spans three generations.

Matthews's grandfather, Clay Matthews, Sr., played four seasons for the San Francisco 49ers in the 1950s. His father, Clay Matthews, Jr., played linebacker for 19 seasons on the Cleveland Browns and the Atlanta Falcons. He was a four-time Pro Bowler. Matthews's uncle, Bruce Matthews, was an offensive lineman, who also played a combined 19 seasons for the Houston Oilers and Tennessee Titans. Uncle Bruce is known as one of the greatest blockers in league history, being voted to an NFL-record-tying 14 Pro Bowls and was inducted into the Pro Football Hall of Fame in 2007.

Once Clay Matthews, Jr., retired, he became the defensive coach for the local high school team in Agoura Hills, California. But this didn't give his son an advantage once he reached high school. His father thought his son needed to get bigger and more physical to be a starter. Matthews grew bigger between his junior and senior season and earned more playing time, but few college recruiters were interested. He decided to enroll at the University of Southern California — where his father and uncle played — and try out for the football team as a walk-on.

Matthews eventually earned a scholarship and played well as a tackler on special teams for the USC Trojans. He continued to work

hard off the field, lifting weights and improving his speed. When USC's defensive coach let Matthews play as a standup defensive end, his improved speed made him hard to block. He led the Trojans in quarterback sacks and caught the attention of NFL scouts.

Specifically, Matthews caught the attention of the Green Bay Packers. They traded draft picks with the New England Patriots to move up and select Matthews with the 26th overall pick of the 2009 NFL Draft.

Even though he was injured during much of his first training camp, Matthews showed his ability to rush the quarterback and chase running backs. Packers' coaches included him in their defensive plans and he played in every regular-season game.

He scored his first NFL touchdown after stripping the ball from a Minnesota Vikings running back on Monday Night Football, and was named Rookie of the Week and month.

Matthews finished his rookie year leading the Packers with 10 quarterback sacks, which was a Packers rookie record. He was also named to the Pro Bowl.

His rookie season was a big success, but Matthews never forgot what it was like to not start for his father at Agoura Hills High. He used that memory to drive him to be even better.

"Even though I'm a first-round pick, a Pro Bowler, I feel like I've never arrived," Matthews said.

Another offseason of hard work and film study helped Matthews play even better in his second NFL season. He played like a veteran, producing 13 ½ sacks, an interception, and a touchdown. He was voted to his second-straight Pro Bowl and finished second to the Pittsburgh Steelers' Troy Polamalu for NFL Defensive Player of the Year.

In the final game of his second season, Matthews stood where every NFL player wants to be: on the Super Bowl field, celebrating an NFL championship.

Troy Polamalu

The All-Pro safety for the Pittsburgh Steelers, Troy Polamalu, is one of the best defensive players to ever play in the NFL. He has helped the Steelers win two Super Bowls since being drafted by the team in 2003.

But Polamalu was not always a big hitter. He was considered small but fast when he played youth football. By the time he played at Douglas High School in Winston, Oregon, he played backup running back and safety on defense.

As Polamalu worked hard and grew larger, he increased his rushing totals to more than 1,000 yards as a sophomore and again as a junior. He also played safety on defense, gaining a reputation for hard tackles on receivers and running backs, and intercepting many passes.

By the time he graduated high school, Polamalu had gained more than 3,100 rushing yards and earned many awards.

After considering scholarship offers from several schools, he chose to attend the University of Southern California. USC coaches liked his football smarts and intensity, and his instinct for knowing where a quarterback was going to throw the ball. He played regularly as a backup his first year with the Trojans and became a starter in his second year. In his third year, Polamalu was named USC's Most Valuable Player.

"He's as good a safety as I ever coached," said Pete Carroll, who coached Polamalu. "He's a brilliant football player. He is creative, fast, tough, and instinctive. He has a great heart, which all great players have."

The first time Carroll saw Polamalu play, the safety blitzed through the offensive line, hit the running back hard enough to knock the ball loose, and ran it in for a touchdown.

He went on to total 278 tackles, had six interceptions, and returned three for touchdowns at USC. He also used his speed to block four punts. He was named a college All-American two times.

The Steelers had their eyes on Polamalu as the 2003 NFL Draft approached. Pittsburgh coaches and staff anxiously waited in hopes that no other team would draft him. The Steelers saw their chance and traded with the Kansas City Chiefs to move up and select Polamalu with the 16th pick.

Polamalu worked hard during his rookie season with the Steelers. He studied opposing quarterbacks and receivers on film for many hours each week, learning their habits and plays. He also was an excellent special-teams player, leading the team in kickoff and punt teams in tackles.

By his second season, he was a fulltime starter and a Pro Bowler. He had a trick for confusing quarterbacks before the snap, faking one formation, then walking with his back to the line. Quarterbacks did not know which receivers or tight ends Polamalu was covering until after the ball was snapped. Polamalu also became feared as a tackler and blitzer, hitting ball carriers and quarterbacks behind the line of scrimmage. He caused many fumbles and interceptions.

During the 2006 season, Polamalu was returning an interception for a touchdown when a running back grabbed his long hair and pulled him to the ground. Grabbing hair is not a penalty in the NFL. Even though it could happen again, Polamalu did not get a haircut.

In 2010, Polamalu was named the NFL's Defensive Player of the Year and helped the Steelers win the AFC championship and a berth in Super Bowl XLV. His jersey was also the best-selling jersey in the NFL.

Even though he's known as a big hitter, Polamalu is also soft-spoken. He has many off-the-field interests including playing the piano and surfing.

It did not take Darrelle Revis long to become one of the best and most feared cornerbacks in the NFL. His reputation has earned him the nickname "Revis Island." The nickname refers to Darrelle being left all by himself — as if alone on an island — to defend against a receiver. He has lived up to his nickname, running side by side with the NFL's best receivers and knocking away passes from the best quarterbacks.

Revis was born into a family of athletes. His mother, Diana Gilbert, was a track star. His uncle is former NFL player Sean Gilbert. When Revis was 12, his uncle Sean helped him work on his strength, speed, and endurance during summer workouts in his home town of Aliquippa, Pennsylvania.

"If you want to be an NFL player," Sean told his nephew, "this is what you need to do to get there."

In high school, Revis was an offensive star. He played quarterback, running back, receiver, cornerback, and kick returner at Aliquippa High School where he earned many Player of the Year honors. Revis led his high school team to the state championship game against Northern Lehigh. He scored an incredible five touchdowns. His unforgettable performance helped lead Aliquippa to a come-from-behind victory and the state title.

Revis also played basketball in high school, leading Aliquippa in scoring and two league championships. He almost accepted a college basketball scholarship offer, but decided that football was his best sport.

His high school accomplishments led many colleges to recruit him. He chose to attend the University of Pittsburgh, where his uncle Sean played college football. Revis contributed immediately as a freshman, playing in every game and earning first-team Freshman All-America honors.

During his three seasons at Pitt, Revis was voted All-Big East twice and nominated for more national awards, including the Jim Thorpe Award for best defensive back and Bronko Nagurski Trophy for best defensive player.

In 2006, Revis's return of a punt for a touchdown was voted the best College Football Play of the Year by ESPN. After catching the punt, Revis ran backward, reversed field, and streaked down the sidelines, breaking several tackles while running 73 yards for a touchdown.

After his junior season at Pitt, Revis entered the 2007 NFL Draft. NFL teams were very interested in his skills at covering opposing receivers and returning kicks and punts. He did not have to wait long on draft day. The New York Jets selected him in the first round with the 14th pick. He became the first Jets rookie cornerback to start a season in more than 10 years and proved the team had made a good decision in drafting him.

With one season under his belt, Revis worked hard during the offseason and showed even more improvement beginning his second NFL season. After he intercepted five passes and was named to the Pro Bowl, teams learned not to throw in his direction.

By the time his third pro season began, Revis earned his reputation as one of the NFL's best cover cornerbacks. He glided side by side with speedy receivers and played bump-and-run coverage against big, physical pass catchers. Revis limited the league's best receivers like Randy Moss and Terrell Owens to just a few catches and yards and was named All-Pro twice.

Jets coach Rex Ryan called Revis the NFL's best cornerback and said he was the best defensive back he has ever worked with.

One thing is for sure, receivers know to stay clear of "Revis Island."

Ndamukong Suh

Big Ndamukong Suh produced an award-winning rookie season, living up to being selected as the second pick in the 2010 NFL Draft.

The top pick of the Detroit Lions, Suh was voted Defensive Rookie of the Year and selected to the Pro Bowl and named All-Pro after finishing with 10 quarterback sacks and 49 tackles. He also intercepted a pass and knocked down three passes.

His journey to the NFL began in Portland, Oregon. Suh's mom was an elementary school teacher and his father once played professional soccer abroad. He has three sisters, the oldest of which played soccer at Mississippi State University.

While attending Grant High School, Suh played offense and defense, excelling on both sides of the ball. As a senior, he had 10 sacks and helped Grant High to the state playoffs. He was also named to national All-America teams.

His high school performance made him the top football recruit in Oregon. After his senior season, he chose to accept a scholarship to play football at the University of Nebraska.

As a college freshman, Suh saw some action, and became a fulltime starter in his second season for the Huskers. In his third season, he became Nebraska's best defensive player, leading the team in tackles and sacks.

By his senior college season, Suh was dominating opposing offensive lines. Forty-four times he stopped a ball carrier at or behind the line of scrimmage. He intercepted a pass, deflected 10 more, and led the Huskers with 12 sacks.

Against the University of Texas in the Big 12 Championship Game, Suh almost single-handedly lifted the Huskers to an upset win with a career-high 12 tackles, 4.5 sacks, and 2 quarterback hurries.

"He was all over the place," Texas coach Mack Brown said. "We just couldn't handle him. I tried to find him to wish him good luck in the NFL because I don't want to see him again."

Suh's unforgettable performance led to his winning many awards including the Bronko Nagurski Trophy, Chuck Bednarik Award, Lombardi Award, and Outland Trophy. He made the biggest headlines as a rare defensive finalist for the Heisman Trophy given to the best college football player each year. Only one defensive player, Charles Woodson from Michigan in 1997, had won the Heisman Trophy. Suh came close, finishing fourth behind the winner, Alabama running back Mark Ingram.

NFL teams who had scouted Suh for a long time were impressed by his abilities. His size, strength, and quickness led the Detroit Lions to make him their first-round pick, second overall, in the 2010 Draft.

Many critics questioned the Lions' decision to draft a defensive tackle with the first pick, but Detroit's coaches and scouts had no doubt about their decision.

Suh began his rookie season as a starter. He recorded his first professional sack in his first NFL game and grabbed his first interception in his fifth game. In his eighth game, after an injury to the team's kicker, Suh even attempted to kick an extra point.

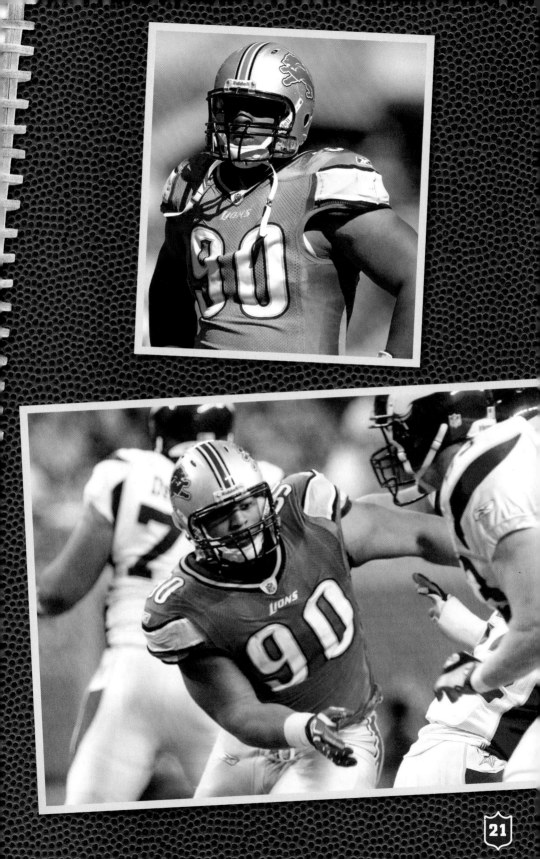

At the season's end, Suh had helped the Lions improve from 2-14 to 6-10 and became the first Detroit rookie to be named a Pro Bowl starter since Hall of Fame running back Barry Sanders.

Cameron Wake

Cameron Wake has taken a very unusual path to becoming an NFL player. Pro scouts and teams did not think Wake was good enough to play professional football, so he quit. Years later, the linebacker proved them all wrong.

Cameron, formerly known as Derek Wake, grew up in Hyattsville, Maryland. While playing basketball for DeMatha High School, he decided to try football. His big size and speed allowed him to excel at his new sport.

He was named the area's Defensive Player of the Year and was visited by legendary Penn State coach Joe Paterno — one of the best college football coaches of all time. Coach Paterno offered him a scholarship to play football and he accepted.

While at Penn State, Wake was a team captain who played linebacker and defensive end. He finished with almost 200 tackles and 8.5 sacks. He ran a fast 40-yard dash time in front of NFL scouts during Penn State's pro day, but did not receive much attention from teams.

After being ignored at the 2005 NFL Draft, Wake signed a rookie free agent contract with the New York Giants, but was released before training camp.

Instead of waiting for another NFL team to call, Wake took a job in a bank. When his job began taking up too much of his workout time, Wake went to work as a personal trainer at a fitness center.

It was at this fitness center where Cameron Wake became who he is today. The fitness center mistakenly put his middle name, Cameron, on his name tag. And the new name stuck! Derek Wake was now Cameron Wake.

With a new identity, Wake could not shake his dream to become a professional football player.

"I'm sitting on the couch watching the game on Sunday, and every game I'm watching and I'm going, 'You know what, I can do that. I'm just as big, as fast, as strong. . . .'" Wake said.

In 2007, Wake joined the British Columbia Lions of the Canadian Football League. He focused on defensive end and immediately caught on, totaling seven tackles and three quarterback sacks in his first game.

Wake finished the season with a league-high 16 sacks and a blocked field goal, becoming the first player in CFL history to be named Rookie of the Year and Most Outstanding Defensive Player in the same season.

The following season, Wake showed that his rookie season was not a fluke, again leading the league in sacks with 23, and being named Most Outstanding Defensive Player in the same season.

In 2009, several NFL teams took notice of Cameron's CFL achievements and made him offers. He chose to play for the Miami Dolphins because he liked the team's organization.

"It wasn't about whoever offered the biggest deal," Wake said. "It was about the coaching staffs, the opportunity, the organizations. Miami put themselves above the others."

Wake was a starter by their fourth game that season. It was a very good debut. He had two sacks, four tackles for a loss, and forced a fumble. He finished the year with 5.5 sacks. He also played on special teams, tackling kick and punt returners.

Opposing offensive linemen feared Cameron's quickness off the line of scrimmage and his speed chasing the ball carrier or getting to the quarterback.

During his second season with the Dolphins, Wake only got better. He was especially hard to block when the Dolphins coaches called for him to blitz the quarterback. He began with 6 sacks in five games and eventually finished third in the NFL with 14 sacks. He was named a Pro Bowl starter and was voted to several All-Pro teams.

Now, every NFL team knows Wake's name and wishes they had drafted him.

Patrick Willis

Patrick Willis is perhaps the best inside linebacker in the NFL. His powerful hits led an opposing receiver to call him "Bam-Bam" because he hits everything. His reputation for working hard and leading his teammates also earned him the nickname "Boss."

Willis began playing football in Bruceton, Tennessee. He played football, basketball, and baseball at Bruceton Central High School. He played linebacker on defense and running back on offense. In his senior season, he rushed for more than 2,000 yards and had 30 touchdowns. On defense, he controlled the line of scrimmage. Willis became the first Tennessee player to win the Mr. Football Lineman Award and Mr. Football Running Back Award in the same season.

Many college coaches were amazed at his size, strength, and quickness, and offered him a football scholarship. When Willis visited the University of Mississippi in Oxford, Mississippi, it reminded him of his hometown. He decided to attend Mississippi, also known as Ole Miss, and enjoyed his classes, making the honor roll in his freshman year.

An injury slowed him during his first two seasons at Ole Miss, but a new coach helped him get into the starting lineup as a junior. Willis started at middle linebacker in his third season, chasing down running backs from sideline to sideline, and blitzing quarterbacks for sacks. Despite playing most of the season with a broken finger, he led the Southeastern Conference (SEC) in tackles and was named first-team All-America and first-team All-SEC.

In his senior season, Willis repeated his league-leading performance, and won national linebacker awards including the Jack Lambert Award and the Dick Butkus Award.

He also continued to succeed in his schoolwork, earning a degree in criminal justice.

During the NFL Combine, Willis showed scouts that he was one of the fastest linebackers in the draft and grabbed the attention of the San Francisco 49ers. The 49ers jumped at the chance to select Willis with the 11th pick of the 2007 NFL Draft and immediately made him a starter.

Willis played as if he was a veteran in his first NFL season, leading the league with 174 tackles and also adding four sacks, two forced fumbles, and five deflected passes. His performance earned him the 2007 NFL Defensive Rookie of the Year and a trip to the Pro Bowl.

"It would be good for people that doubted, or didn't know if you could be a No. 1 draft pick, or if you could come into the league and do well because of your size . . . and show them that if you put your mind to it, you're capable of anything," Willis said.

In his second NFL season, Willis scored his first pro football touchdown, returning an interception 86 yards for a score. He ranked second in NFL tacklers and was voted to the Pro Bowl for a second straight year.

Willis became only the second 49ers player to be elected to the Pro Bowl in each of their first four seasons.

He continued to lead the league in tackles into his fifth pro season. His performance earned him a contract extension with the 49ers that made him the highest-paid inside linebacker in the NFL.

Willis helped the 49ers improve to playoff contenders and promises to continue to be the "Boss" on the field for seasons to come.